SAUDADE
Thirty Poems of Longing

poems by

Elizabeth Varadan

Finishing Line Press
Georgetown, Kentucky

SAUDADE
Thirty Poems of Longing

ACKNOWLEDGMENTS

Many thanks to fellow poets in three groups who have given advice and
support for my poetry: The Tuesday Night Poetry Group, moderated by
Danyen Powell, The Wednesday Poetry Group, moderated by Norma
Kohout and Joyce Odam, the online poetry group, Courante Verse,
moderated by Angela Felsted. You have helped me on my journey.

Thanks, too, to June Augusta Gillam and friends in Portugal, Marisa Rocha,
Carla Pereira, and Joana Prata, for reading early drafts of this collection and
giving their feedback.

Publisher: Leah Maines
Editor: Christen Kincaid
Cover Art: Rajan Varadan
Author Photo: Rajan Varadan
Cover Design: Elizabeth Maines McCleavy

Printed in the USA on acid-free paper.
Order online: www.finishinglinepress.com
also available on amazon.com

Author inquiries and mail orders:
Finishing Line Press
P. O. Box 1626
Georgetown, Kentucky 40324
U. S. A.

Table of Contents

This book is for my husband
and for our friends in Portugal

SAUDADE #1

A yearning for
what was lost,
what could have been
but was stillborn.

A reaching for the
unreachable,
what cannot be
but might have been.

Oh, the unattained and
unattainable!
Oh, the trembling hopes
and dashed dreams!

Saudade.

PESSOA

When the poems were found bundled,
inside a trunk,
the poet was dead.

The poems wanted to get out.
They yearned to be
spoken, sung, read.

He shaped them as personas who
conversed, had dialogues
inside his head.

Poems cannot be silenced. Longing
comes from the soul. Poems
transcend and spread.

The poet is gone, yes.
He has slipped away.
His poems live on instead.

ANCIENT GREEKS

Ancient Greeks knew *saudade*.

Heraclitus understood
you cannot enter the
same river twice.
All is flux.
The past permutes,
into a vanishing point.
Nothing can be as it was.

Zeno's Achilles still cannot
overtake the tortoise
as they race toward
a shrinking infinity.
The future beckons; we
advance, but the distance
cannot be closed.

No return. No arrival. Only *saudade*.

FADO

The trembling tones of a
fado linger on the air. They
make a hole in the heart and
drench my soul with sorrow.
Yearning lies captive
in the tremulous timbre of
the singer's voice.
Each turn of phrase
speaks loss, softly
echoing between notes
from the *fadista's* throat.

THE FIRST TIME I HEARD FADO

At a restaurant with friends
on an open patio,
looking up, I saw the moon—
a swollen, full moon
hanging silver in the black night.
We waited.

Against the restaurant wall,
a platform glowed luminescent
from green lamplight.
A door opened.
We waited.

Two musicians entered,
one with Portuguese guitar,
one with classical. Both
strummed their instruments.
We waited.

Slowly the *fadista* walked out,
her gown and shawl
black to match the night;
to match the notes soon
pouring forth
in lament.

THE OPERA OF FADO

Fado is like opera.
Each tells a story.
ending in tears from
thwarted lives or in
laughter at absurd ones.

Opera or *fado*—
both resonate with
destiny's lost dreams.
Yet they tell the story
in differing ways:

In opera, each aria,
singer by singer,
advances the plot,
In *fado*, an entire opera is
distilled into a single song.

AMALIA

"Estranha forma de vida . . .."
("Strange form of life . . ..")
Her voice conveyed
the sad arias and
bright moments from the
opera that was
her life.

Vibrato of pain,
soaring cry of despair,
rise and fall of story,
sweetness, humor—
and always the
longing.

"Strange form of life . . .."
In an old, flickering
newsreel they carried the
casket out, while musicians
wept, crowds wept,
I wept.

I, TOO

I, too, look back,
nostalgic for lost dreams.
I, too, walk forward
toward an unknown destiny.

In memory, I sift through pain
of those who slipped away
too early, and mourn their
unborn second chances.

But death cannot be undone.
I mourn their unmet dreams,
their defeats. I long for their
redemptive outcomes.

SAUDADE #2

Saudade can take
you by surprise.
Sudden memory in
the midst of laughter
can twist the heart,

casting shadows
into the future
until hopes lie
with folded wings,
their flight denied.

BURNING

Another day burns away,
the page curling at the edges.
Gray creeps toward the center.
Lost sentiments rise in smoke wisps—
old messages that once were plans.

They vanish, word by word,
fragmenting, scattering into the air
where each letter flutters,
an inarticulate yearning
of the heart.

WAITING

Between departure
and arrival, there is
only the reaching,
inhabiting the space
and time where
expectations freeze
to a standstill
of waiting.

A regret of loss
haunts the journey
that may or may not
happen. We look
back to a disappeared
past, to a future
that may vanish.
And we wait.

VEIL OF TEARS

Through a veil of tears
the past reverberates
with scenes that might
have been different.

They distill into one image:
I see you wandering,
confused and hopeless,
and I unable to help.

Through a veil of tears
I long to reach back,
rcshape your world,
though this cannot be.

I hear your silent weeping,
stopped in the throat,
locked in your heart,
locked in your endless night.

IF I COULD CHANGE TIME

If I could change time,
I would stretch minutes
to hours, hours to years
full of soft words
and understanding.

Why do we understand
only after a moment
has fled into the
irrevocable past
for which we long?

If I could change time,
I would shrink aimless
talk, empty quarrels,
all harsh words to
a fleeting second.

Ah, but time's flow is
irreversible. Regrets
strewn along the way
mingle their residue
with the longing.

REGRET

Regret is a bitter fruit,
a poisoned apple of
diminished hopes
that paralyze the tongue
and ache the heart.
Ingest it in small splinters,
lest the heart shut down.

CHOICES

If you leave the past,
it shadows you.
Yet, the future haunts as well
with untaken paths.

The leap forward may be
over a cliff's edge.
Safe dreams may only yield
a circumscribed life.

Blind to the unknown,
stay or go—
either is a risk.

FEAR

The hand of fear
closes around my heart,
its icy grip
unkind to dreams.

Terror shivers
through the mirage
of hope, pressing
vitality out of illusion.

Chimeras yield
to awareness,
fear's harsh residue
of wisdom.

Only then comes courage.
Only then comes decision.

DOORS

When one door closes, another
opens. Which door do you close?
Which do you open?

Do you turn your back on a
past shaped by
moments of meaning?
Leave it behind to leap
the precipice of promise?

Do you close off a future
of beguiling dreams
to cherish familiar ground
laced with memories?

Loss and longing lie
across each threshold.

SAUDADE #3

Saudade is a word that hovers on
the tongue and twists the heart
with tangled strands of longing,
pulling the soul one way and another.

Saudade is a longing that
can never be fulfilled.
Our dreams elude us.
Our losses haunt us.

Between dreams and loss,
saudade parades new phantoms
of promise, making us long anew.

MY TROUBLED LAND

My troubled land afflicts my heart.
The body politic is crucified by
daggers of hate, leaving a wake of
pain and sorrow in the name of faith.

My troubled land grieves my soul.
Seams that once held firm are slit, the
social fabric torn by credos that
condone heartless destruction.

My troubled land gives me anguish.
Scenes of tyranny abound. Fissures
web the nation. The greedy mock
those in need and those who care.

Weep, my troubled land!
I long for better times.
Weep.

THE LOSS OF MY LAND

I lament the loss
of my land.

Sometimes land is taken
from you, but it can
vanish before your eyes
by degrees.

The land of my childhood
is vanishing, nibbled
and crippled by a deep
soul disease:

Those who cared for others
are scorned, compassion
smothered by hate, fear,
and greed.

I lament the loss
of my land.

HOW CAN IT HAVE COME TO THIS?

How can it have come to this?

People live in
dread of loss,
displacement,
bodily harm.
Bonds have shredded.
Trust has fled,
ideals smashed in
an anarchy of spite.

How can it have come to this?

WHEN I LOOK BACK

When I look back,
and walk the streets of memory

I see each vanished face.
I feel again
the helping hands
along life's way.
I breathe again
the sense of hope and
vanquished despair.
My younger self
reaches out,
touching grace.

Grace has departed now.
The streets we walk bode ill.

IF MY HEART IS HEAVY

If my heart is heavy, it is
because the powerful shrug off
tragedy afar when once they
would have been moved.

If my heart is heavy,
it is because cynicism greets the
innocent, scoffing against the
efficacy of love.

If my heart lifts, it is because
protagonists in this sad *fado*,
struggle for justice to prevail,
for fellowship to heal,
for heart to meet heart once again.

DESTINY

We reach for stars
and destiny intervenes.
Around the curve of
the road, destiny awaits,
an earthen path,
strewn with rocks and
fallen branches, leading
to streams of surprise
with no bridges.
Only the longing.
Only the reaching for stars.

DREAMS

Dreams are golden edges
of despair's cloud.
Hope limns the periphery,
gleaming, beckoning,
reminding us that,
while hidden,
beyond lies the longing
that never fades.

NIGHT

Night falls, drawing a curtain
across another day of longing
for a kinder vision.
The moon travels its lonely
path, lost among stars.
The stars keep their distance
in the dark, silent night.
Constellations wheel round in
the abyss of space.
And I, at the window,
yearn for signs of promise in
the new break of day.

MY FATE

Like a tree lifting
supplicant branches,
I stretch out my hands
to my fate.
A breeze stirs leaves
of longing for what is
yet to come.
Oh come, future moment;
hasten to my side,
bringing the fate
that awaits me.

PATTERNS

Black lace trees fan out against
a red sunset, spreading
patterns across the horizon.

My heart pulses with expectation
and a little fear of what
hopes can camouflage.

Does longing hide dreams or destiny?
Is waiting mirage or realization?
The patterns overlay mysteries I cannot solve.

DAWN

Dawn brings new dreams.
Soft hues suffuse morning clouds
with brightness when the sun
slowly appears.

Come, sweet sunrise, come
in gentle shades of pink and gold.
Fade the gray of night
with yesterday's disappointed hopes.
Edge the horizon with possibility.
Outshine grief and loss
with new longing.

SAUDADE #4

A barren heart
has given up longing.
Loss can carve your soul,
leaving unhealing wounds.

Yet the harrowed heart
longs for seeds of hope
to be sown, for the
plant of bounty to flourish.

Saudade can keep the heart
dormant, waiting to trust again.

A FEW NOTES AND DEFINITIIONS

Saudade—"Saudade" is best explained in the first poem: it is an adjective that doesn't translate easily into English. The nearest definition is "longing", but it goes beyond that. It's a sense of thwarted dreams, a sense of fate intersecting with your longings. Friends have pointed out that it can be a sense of nostalgia (a happier sense of longing), as well.

Fado—Sometimes this art form has been called the Portuguese "blues". And, like the blues, Fado is haunting and does convey an outpouring of emotion about the challenges of life. But the melodies are quite different from traditional American blues; and the lyrics could, in my opinion, stand alone as beautiful poems. The word "Fado" actually means "Fate".

Fadista—A Fado singer. A fadista can be either male or female. The women traditionally wear black and are accompanied by two guitarists, one on acoustical guitar, and one on Portuguese guitar (which somewhat resembles the Greek Bouzouki, but is slightly different.) Music is always evolving, however, and some contemporary fadistas now include whole orchestras as background for their beautiful songs.

Amalia—A leading 20th century fadista who became famous worldwide. She is often referred to as the "queen of fado"; and my husband and I have several of her CDs and think her title is well deserved.

Pessoa—Fernando Pessoa, a 20th century Portuguese poet, is one of Portugal's two most famous poets. (The other is Luís Vaz de Camões, a 16th century poet who is famous for his epic poem, *The Lusiads*.) Pessoa was quite an original and created literary personas with whom to write different types of poetry and literary criticism. (They even critiqued each other's' works!)

Elizabeth Varadan is a former elementary teacher who writes for both children and adults. She was born in Reno, Nevada, but her family traveled a lot, mainly in California, so she considers herself a Californian at heart. She holds a BA from University of California, Berkeley (History Major, English Minor), as well as a Standard Elementary Teaching Credential from San Francisco State University.

Published work for children includes an MG mystery involving Sherlock Holmes, *Imogene and the Case of the Missing Pearls* (MX Publishing, 2015), a picture book, *Dragonella*, (Belanger Books, 2016; Spanish Edition, 2017), and a collection of stories for children ages 7 to 70, *The Carnival of the Animals* (Belanger Books, 2018).

Adult short stories and flash fiction have appeared in several online and print magazines, including T*he Rockford Review, Word Riot, Art Times, Flash Me Magazine, Long Story Short, Page & Spine, Epiphany, Melic Review*, and a story, "Kidnapped" was included in the 2016 Sherlock Holmes related story collection, *Beyond Watson* (Belanger Books, 2016).

Her poetry has appeared in *Song of the San Joaquin, The Ophidian, The Stray Branch, Vine Leaves Literary Journal, Poems for all-Little Book*s, and her poem, "Return to India", was selected as an International Merit Award winner in the *Atlanta Review* 2017 International Poetry Competition.

She and her husband live in Midtown Sacramento, California. They have traveled to India many times, where her husband was born. In recent years, they divide travel time between Braga, Portugal, and Trasulfe, Galicia (an autonomous region in Spain), both places that inspire her fiction and poetry. *Saudade, Thirty Poems of Longing*, is her first chapbook. Currently she is working on a cozy mystery series set in Braga, Portugal and a second chapbook of poems about Galicia, Spain.

www.ingramcontent.com/pod-product-compliance
Lightning Source LLC
LaVergne TN
LVHW051611080426
835510LV00020B/3237